6/80

Where Is Mortimer?

Karen Bryant-Mole

Gareth Stevens Publishing
MILWAUKEE

Mortimer's Math

For a free color catalog describing Gareth Stevens' list of high-quality books and multimedia programs, call 1-800-542-2595 (USA) or 1-800-461-9120 (Canada). Gareth Stevens Publishing's Fax: (414) 225-0377.

Library of Congress Cataloging-in-Publication Data available upon request from publisher. Fax: (414) 225-0377 for the attention of the Publishing Records Department.

ISBN 0-8368-2622-1

This North American edition first published in 2000 by
Gareth Stevens Publishing
1555 North RiverCenter Drive, Suite 201
Milwaukee, WI 53212 USA

This edition © 2000 by Gareth Stevens, Inc. Original © BryantMole Books, 1999. First published as *Where is Marmaduke?* by Evans Brothers Limited, 2A Portman Mansions, Chiltern Street, London W1M 1LE, United Kingdom. Additional end matter © 2000 by Gareth Stevens, Inc.

Created by Karen Bryant-Mole
Photographs by Zul Mukhida
Designed by Jean Wheeler
Teddy bear by Merrythought Ltd.

Printed in the United States of America

1 2 3 4 5 6 7 8 9 04 03 02 01 00

E

175

1. Prepositions

I. T

contents

behind

Where is Mortimer
the bear?

He is hiding behind
a vase of flowers.
Can you see him
peeking out?

Hello, Mortimer!

Mortimer is
sitting in front
of the vase
of flowers.

Now you can
see all of me.

up

Mortimer is climbing up the slide.

Look at me, way up here.

down

Mortimer slides
down to the bottom.

Whee!
That was fun!

on

Mortimer is pretending
to be in a circus.
He is balancing
on a ball.

Look at me!

off

Oh, dear!
Mortimer has fallen off the ball.

Ouch!

in

Mortimer is sitting
in a bucket.
What a funny
place to sit!

out

Mortimer is getting out of the bucket.

That bucket was not very comfortable!

over

Mortimer is
having fun.
He is jumping
over a rope.

This is hard
to do!

under

Mortimer has thought of something different to try. Now he is crawling under the rope.

This is much easier!

inside

Can you find Mortimer?
He is hiding inside the box.
You can just see his eyes
and his nose.

outside

Now Mortimer is outside the box.

It was dark inside the box, but it is light outside the box.

above

Mortimer is standing above a toy car.

If I look down, I can see the car.

Mortimer
is standing
below a ball.

I have to
look up to see
the ball.

beside

Mortimer is standing beside his basket of building blocks.

The blocks are next to me.

through

Mortimer has built an archway with his blocks. He is walking through the archway.

I am walking from one side to the other.

between

Mortimer is sitting between two toy cars.

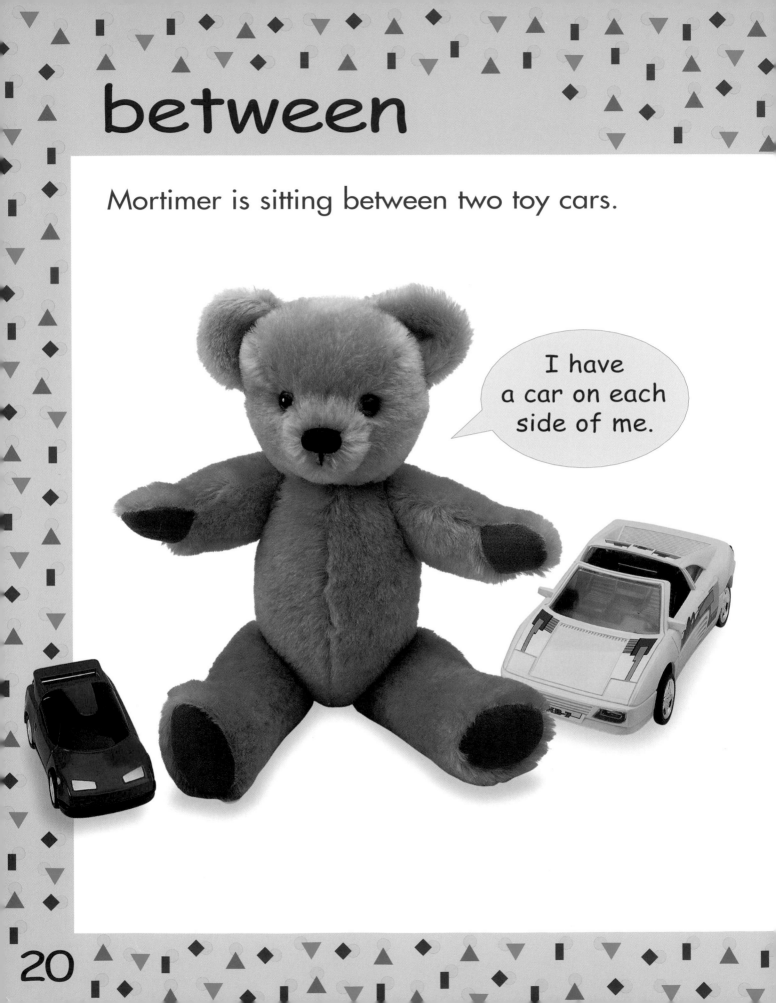

I have a car on each side of me.

among

Mortimer is playing with all his cars.
He is sitting among the cars.

There are cars all around me.

21

Where is Mortimer?

Mortimer can use different words to describe where he is sitting.

I am sitting on a bucket, between two watering cans.

glossary/index

archway — a doorway or an entrance with a curved top that people can walk through 19

balancing — staying on top of something that is wobbly or hard to stand on without falling off 8

circus — a traveling show that has clowns, acrobats, animals, and other performers 8

comfortable — being at ease; feeling good 11

describe — to use words to explain or tell about something 22, 23

hiding — staying out of sight 4, 14

peeking — looking out from behind something in a quick or secret way 4

pretending — playing "make believe;" acting like or claiming to be something or someone else 8

vase — an open container used to hold flowers 4, 5

videos

Clifford's Fun With Opposites. (Scholastic)

Get Ready for Math. (Western Publishing Co.)

Math Is Fun series. (Great Plains National Instructional Library)